Leave Me
a
Little Want

Also by Beverly Burch

POETRY
Latter Days of Eve
How a Mirage Works
Sweet to Burn

NONFICTION
Other Women
On Intimate Terms

Leave Me
a
Little Want

Terrapin Books

Terrapin Books
4 Midvale Avenue
West Caldwell, NJ 07006

www.terrapinbooks.com

ISBN: 978-1-947896-58-1
Library of Congress Control Number: 2022941601

First Edition

Cover art: *Suspended*, Photograph, 2022
by Ellie Waxman

Cover design: Diane Lockward

Contents

So in this great disaster of our birth
We can be happy, and forget our doom.

—George Santana, Sonnet XXV

Rumors of the Solitary Pulse

You feel the world as a weight?
It's all that heavy air. Even a sparrow's song
creates a little pressure.
Once you were snugged inside
a small organ. Fed without opening your mouth,
no need to work those precious lungs.

Tiny jellyfish, how your arms waved.
Buoyant legs punted a soft wall.
But the bud of the mind kept unfurling,
pushing you toward the world.
O startling light, skip and jig of voices,
honeyed touch of flesh.

Rigged for reception, you were ready.
Then the presence of air did you in.
How separate you felt.

Born-Again Sonnet

At first I could only dream. Then language came
and I threaded dubious words together, strands
my mother wore proudly. Small explorer, I went after
words. For years, brought them in from the wild.
That treacherous province, like a jungle, doesn't thrive
with such treatment. It loses its savage gleam,
leaves only a lawn, tidy and precise. No more swarm,
no rain forest threatening the village, just radios
blaring the commonplace. Taken from primeval mud,
what you unearth wastes away. There is no cure.
Today my dreams come in unknown tongues.
How can I understand them? Who can I tell them to?
I wait for a new paradise, land without improvement
where speech is green and wordless.

Riddle

What large mysteries roamed the house.
What creatures sang by the hearth, arms and legs rocking.
Whose flesh fed you, whose hands lifted you
when voices chorused inside.

Who revealed your name. Who said, this is your food,
this is how we drink. Whose look stirred you, sly turn
over the shoulder, the side-eye. Whose kiss assuaged you
after long drought.

Whose body imprinted you. Who planted flags,
claimed territory, subjugated your culture. What did the natives
know. How did the language evolve to hushed intonation,
sharp-clicked tongue.

Whose rules mimed the cadence of gods.
What flawed histories seduced you. Why did no one
unravel the codes.

Who dropped the silk thread out the door,
down the sidewalk as you left for parts unknown,
explorer and refugee. Who made sure you'd return.

How did they tether you. Who were they really.

Autobio in Scent Memory

Gardenias again. Is it August? Atlanta.
In steaming darkness I abandoned my grandmother
to a back room, big bed. She was sinking, it was the end.
Down flagstone steps to trade dirty jokes
with the boys.

Charred smell of scorched brakes. Remember
my parents' faces, mute fury. How they hurled my
new keys into the hedge. Background music,
neighbor's scratchy Miles Davis.

Firethorn's odor, carrion-like. Flies love it.
Cluster of red berries, red cyanic fruit. It was a three-room flat,
me and a man who strayed, wept, strayed, wept.
We hung on through the rot that April.

Wood smoke, campfire, lovely stale cigarette smoke—
a woman I met a month ago, lean, dark-haired,
and her van, the Sierra, kisses
like butterscotch, rush of Ponderosa.

Whiff of diesel. Everywhere in Asuncion ancient buses
heave down boulevards. I carried a baby
along tiled sidewalks. Adoption lawyer,
tiny courtroom. I couldn't stop pacing.
Heat, glare. *Lapachos* in bloom.

Antiseptics, that disturbing reek. Slight trace brings back
crisp voices, clatter of little tools. A new lump
near the jawbone. The vinyl pad
was so sweaty, I was so sweaty, reading to her
with an anesthetic hum. Shoes *mooshed* along linoleum.
One doctor wouldn't stop talking.
Excruciating countdown, then the good news.

Ars Poetica with Geometrics

Where there is matter, there is geometry.
—Johannes Kepler

Simple straight line erupts into promise.
It rounds, embraces itself, creates a circle,
room for a world inside. It implodes
to a period, draws the matter to a tiny black hole.
It splits in two, each part travels the same
way, whistles the same tune,
almost hand in hand but never touching.
Coupled, attracted to each other, allure
of parallel lives. They tangle, track back twice
and re-twine, a love knot, looped into joy.
One half intersects the other, a plus.
And at the cross, resurrection happens.
Split again, four parts square off, a quatrain,
a box, spacious as the circle, gift-ready.
Angles alter, veer off on a lark, opposite points
tug at each other. Rhombus, rhythm, rhumba.
Tension. They swing apart again, back and forth
switchback up a path. Fall, fracture,
realign, six sides of uncertain pursuit.
Prismatic, polygonal, form that doesn't want
to stop breaking, realigning, breaking, realigning.
Where's it going and what's it after?
Apeirogon, countable and infinite in one figure.
Vast simplicity, a humble line.

Loose Sonnet

If the car spins out in a halo of lights
or the plane drops with a spiraling whine,
could we please have a moment to loosen
the stays, let this too-dangerous flesh fall away?
I'd like to learn how, wear my skin
like a loose suit. The way timber truck drivers
careen twenty-ton loads through the Bitterroots,
one leg at the door, poised to leap.
If Sufis slip from the body, cross the Al-Dahna
at noon, there must be a zipper,
a soul-shaped crack. Blessed aperture,
please let us out easy. Wasn't it enough
that we came in bloody, everything screaming,
that we were stupefied by light?

Incantation to an Evanescent Self

Each rattled head of tall grass, each green blade
in the meadow quakes, vanishes in the herd
as wind tows it into motion. One undulating ripple
and singularity disappears. What if you're that dispersible,
no star quality to send you center stage?
Unadorned, unnoticed as a winter tree.

You might as well exhale into the afternoon glitter,
let that old craving explode like a glass pellet.
Try, catch an exhilarating glimpse—
yourself, pixelated, then gone. Starburst, atoms that mingle
such a short time. It doesn't really hurt, does it?

Uncertain Sonnet

How did you imagine you'd taken up the cello?
You felt the burnished curves between your legs,
wood like satin. Surprised, your skilled fingers
plucked strings, arm arced the bow like a longtime
lover. Intimacy of released sound—not inside,
not outside, at the juncture. You've never touched
a cello, but feel this music, these strokes as if
you stirred a past life. Or unknown ancestor surfaced—
her flat in nineteenth-century Berlin trembling
with lost sonatas. Like the day you waded
in woodland water, watched leaves spin
idle dreams and felt someone nearby. A cave,
sacred fire, urge to gather willow sticks, green herby
things, cochineal berries. No clue what or why.

Post Haste

The line at the P.O. is seven deep.
Two clerks slow-waltz the weighing and stamping
like acolytes of an ancient ballet master,
choreographer of arms that halt midair, hover,
trail sedately to the scale. Their eyes gaze blankly
at the audience. Slothful swans.

In fifteen minutes I'm due across town.
It takes ten to drive.
Squeezing days into crevices of time,
I triumph in feats of efficiency.

Only one clerk now. She eyes me twice,
pauses before sliding another package toward eternity.
Possibly she rooted here twenty years ago,
gave up on release.

There could be a practice in it:
the novice patiently sweeping around the bodhi tree.
Fine difference. Enlightenment or torpid trance.
Equally hypnotic, the hurry and dash,

my daily fugue. It's a steady descent,
sentience tumbling into a chasm.

Mad Sonnet

Driving home, Gillian Welch on a playlist
singing *Annabelle*, a song about a lost child.
Blue twang of her alto's a pure swell, mad sorrow
that licks up the air. Steering gets harder,
like I'm moving through sludge, heaviness
wheels can't handle. Maybe it's the rain,
how light's fled from the day, road difficult to see.
Or the song set free a bottled-up genie.
What she feels, I feel it too, barely surviving.
I never buried a child, but now I have.
Like when I listen to Omora sing Butterfly,
her voice pins me to my chair. I feel myself lift
the dagger, ready to plunge. I never worry I'll
do myself in for love. Then I could, I'm there.

Rumors of the Old Somewhere

Names disappeared here with faces.
Vacancy on hearthstones, kudzu blinding window panes.
A leafy orchard where initials necklace the trees.

Did we live here once? Sometimes a mother takes us back
to visit. We stumble along tire tracks
headed into the woods. Ruined corn stalks, a chewed up
pair of red sandals. Did we read about this place?

Remember how the dogs trapped an old possum
in the cistern, how the terrified animal starved in there?
We swept that kitchen floor, buried the week's garbage.
How we cried when the cat's mouth
held blue feathers.

Did someone tell us about this place?
Have some of us taken our mothers there?

In the spring crabapple blossoms litter gravestones
and sun falls through poplars like fool's gold.
Red autumn rains down in torrents.
Each winter a skeletal army of trees inches forward
before the fires come.

Restless Sonnet

Just try to make the mind lie down like a good dog.
It barks whenever wind hits the bushes.
It wants a rabbit, a mouthful of flesh in its teeth,
warm scoop of blood. Wants to tangle with the neighbor's
trash, rub its nose in something rotten. Hyped-up
on possibility, it settles for its own tail. Tie a kerchief to its tail,
it runs in circles half an hour. Oh, won't that crazy dog tire?

Squirrels snicker in the poplars, the cat rolls with hilarity.
That slows the poor pooch. It's why we keep
the cat. Bright notions sift through the blinds.
She stares them down. Isn't she the furry little Buddha,
curled on her silk pillow? Radical non-effort.
Look in her eyes—do you see shame?
She snuffs out the foolish mind, twenty hours a day.

Elegy with Bereft Cat

Mac, a tawny beast with devotional eyes, sits at the French doors
and whimpers. Outside lies the garden path, sunbaked flagstones, Eden.

Flash of hummingbirds in lantern bush and lorapetalum.

He snatched his third last week, so house arrest now. Those days, I tell him,
are over. Such mewling grief.

Once I couldn't bear to lack what I wanted: it hones your insides
like a boning knife. Three lovers in one week,
I felt neither shame nor doubt. And other missteps I can't speak of.

Age comes like a scourge: red-hot with renunciation.
Today I lingered outside, the light in the trees
almost not bearable. Intensity. More subtle than passion.

Odd to be grateful so much of my life is over.

Mac's all instinct and he pays. In another year he'll be contented.
A lap, walk-around, a chase. Eager for a spinning thing, fresh can of salmon.

Sprung Sonnet

You grew morose as dogwoods, azaleas opened.
A blight on your spirit, spring. Too smart,
you knew the blinding snare of blossoms,
how opulence beguiles and betrays.
Myself, I fell for it year after year, flinging wide
the net when scented air stirred. Warmth, roses!
Defenseless, southern heat broke me,
parched me. I learned to crave a chill.
The sheer breath of desire, I panted for October.
As animals thickened their fur, I slowly unbolted
the portal to nature again. Yes, red lies hung
on maple trees, the golden oaks were fraudulent.
Initiated now, I know perfection winks
for only a moment, summoning before it smites.

Incantation for a Hard Rain

.

Days the sky uncorked and sopped us through
we ran, we swore. Then drought, hills dusty
as moth wing, primeval forests sickened.
O tempests, come back. Bring your pelting fury
to the fields, batter the fat leaves of the poplars.
School us to stand real weather. The willows took it
like saints and martyrs, swayed and moaned
as they were thrashed. Towhees hunkered down,
bush rabbits, fragile spiders endured.
Heaven of cloudy billows, send us a gray devil.
No weak sister. Don't slap us with hope and disappear.
Teach us to grow lyrical as we're assailed.

Ars Poetica with Literary Executions

If you can still hear your fear, shift a gear.
—anonymous biker

At the open mic an author says, *While these poems
make little sense, it won't kill you to listen.*
True crime affairs, the first stanzas have victims,
all of them in the audience, and you begin to feel nervous.

Someone's sonnet slays someone. The slain person gets up,
reads their own shiftless ode and someone else perishes.
On and on, a miniseries. The crowd clamors for poetic justice,
making anapests of themselves to keep the rhythm going.

Atrocities are also routine among the critics. Suddenly, transport
arrives. Motorcycles rev outside. *Just read loud,*
the emcee says. You go to the mic, mutter about choppers,
how many people give their lives to the ride. You mean poems.

You know they're vehicles for anxiety, their risky *vroom-vroom,*
vigorous throaty calls roaming the crest of the unknown.
You don't sight them at first, just hear their rumble. For a moment
you're close, you hop on. For a moment it's your turn to ride.

Incantation Against Blazing

Three a.m. bolt of panic hits, thoughts of disaster
to come. You spring out of bed, blazed by adrenaline,
transfixed by the body's power to destroy.
Everything that matters in that moment
lies in the word *relief*. Then the feeling passes.

Remember, driving down I-5 from Oregon, steep grade
through the Shasta Cascade. You saw a Winnebago
sprout flames from its rear brakes.
You leaned on the horn. Everyone leaned
on their horns. The heavy wheels flew downhill,
family inside. On a long curve you heard the explosion,
saw the thing flattened, black as a charred cake.

Of course you remember. The flaming load
of the past careens on, disguised as the future
at three a.m. Back to bed. You've seen things that
branded you, more than just that,
but as far as you know someone found relief.

Busted Sonnet

My mother, my devoted one, had her limits.
It was weep at your own risk. It was ridicule by song.
If I teared up, she crooned, *She's a real sad tomato,*
a busted Valentine. What was I to do with scorn
but collect other mothers, listeners and consolers,
fan wavers, hand-holders. Schoolmarms embraced me
like madonnas. Little favor here, kind words there.
I turned to neighbors, an auntie, piano teacher,
gathered beads for my rosary, wore its prayer.
Her aim was true. *Dear female child, I'll toughen you.*
What if at last her stomach churned, had enough
of this work. Poor brain, etched by acidic tools,
impulses fleeing down the same neuronal path.
I ran blind up the hallway, her voice in pursuit.

Hollow Bones

Gingko, its quivering leaves, bird-like,
frightened on their hollow bones, fanned over us
as we poured wine into Dixie Cups,
a bargain red, the few ounces you could handle.
No actual birds around, silent as they are
mid-afternoon, only those leaves, trapped
and fluttering on memory's thin stalks.
In that uprooted city, it was good
to have an ancient relic above us.
You would have stayed all day if you could.
The next year I drove past not wanting to look.
October had stunned the tree. Leaves like a flock
of gold, broadcasting to a listening sky.
New moon crooked a skinny finger overhead:
spread those ashes. Chastised, I returned at dawn
with my ceramic pot. The poor tree was naked,
a total overnight drop. They do that.
Maidenhair, bald now.
What would you think if I left you there anyway?
I did, with relief. Scattered you in its blond debris.
False medicine in gingko, I read.
Its extract does not heal body or mind.
Does not improve memory. It jolts memory.
I planted one in my yard. This morning I saw it,
like an old scarecrow, yellow pooled at its feet.
I flinched. Foolish body, speaking like that.
The ashes were a mistake. I have not released you.

Unholy Sonnet

Do you not know your body is a temple?
           —Corinthians 6:19

Some days it's all effluvia and blood soak.
Some days tongues speak so dirty they need soaping.
Sweet tumescent tissues beg for transgression. Ignorant of prayer,
the body croons, it wanders over the ridge, eyes grazing
on lupine, poppies. What a vehicle, this delectable flesh,
a shape-shifting carriage for distracted souls. What a vessel,
canvas wailing for its paint. What a pail of slop, what a culvert.
Sea surge tosses salt into lungs, brines the body's juices.
Flesh bends thinking one way, heart another.
They arrive at the same place, puffing like an old bellows,
recalling spring clouds of jasmine, wisteria.
Body never quite makes it to heaven. A handful of ashes,
homesick, scattered in the desert. Or silent in the boneyard,
unholy tissues offered to grateful larvae. Still, a song.

Rumors of Ecuador and Elephants

check out a cross-section: ivory
creamy white tusks   sliced open
intersecting chevrons   organic geometry

in a parable   sightless men   handle an elephant
one stroking the lengthy trunk   one   a barrel leg
one   a wide flank   each insists

the others describe   the wrong animal
how to see   a whole animal? ropy tail   great flop
of ear   bristled maw with shining hooks

Ecuadorean tribes   share dreams   at daybreak
fit them into   an elegant puzzle   the real dream
a daily packet   posted by the gods

bracelets   piano keys   scrimshaw   sculpture
all of them   butchered beasts   a sequel
to our not knowing   how to dream

our tribe   we hold tight
each with our own slice   little to see
infinity waiting   for an open hand

Mortal Absence

Countryside in winter. Too much absence here.
I've gone too long without speaking and seen no one for days.
      Even the wind carries the scent
of desolation. I start thinking catastrophe,
like I'm a sole survivor.
      Reality swerves on thin ice.

City mayhem tempers the mind.
Irascible horns, flashing lights, music thumping
      out someone's window.
Here, nothing but silence. Until a small furor in a bare hedge
      hardly noticed, unhinges me again—
a shadow falls and wind whistles to an upward draft.
      In the bush, a hermit thrush, bird she loved,

flaps leaves around. It feels like presence.
      Hair at the back of my neck bristles.
I shake a little, new shock, the bird's watching, witching me.
Or it's her. I can't tell. Just feel her brightness,
      quick rush of molecules.

It's how I miss her. How the missing brings her
      back to life. Then a cold dose of fear.
Yes, she misses me too. She wants me with her.
I don't want to be with her. I mean, I do,
      but not enough. That's how she makes
the world roar back again.

Erratic Sonnet

Tinnitus: madness in the ears. Static pulsing.
The saturated hum of outer space. After loud noises—
a siren, jackhammer, garbage man—tinnitus goes wild:
electronic bees, enraged. A hive in uproar,
the queen furious. High wires in a strong wind, singing.
Droning, a monitor when the heart flatlines.

I remember quiet. Lying on red rock
in the middle of Utah. Sky changed its attitude,
bedrock kept silent. Lengthening hush like darkness
in a middle-of-nowhere night. Not even silent retreats
are that silent. In meditation halls there's a sniffle,
crack of a lower back, heavy breathers. Listen now:
constant buzz, my familiar. An earful.
Subtle rhythm, subtle din, then pure shrill sound.

Seven A.M.

Every act of rebellion expresses nostalgia for innocence...
—Albert Camus

Curl tighter. The street's thick murmur—
even rocked in the womb you heard it.
Refuse to slide out.
Unfurl your flag of revolt.
Do nothing, be one lazy beast, you
who itched with ambition.
The world's as muted as it ever gets.
Later you'll raise
the blind's eye. O later please,
you don't want to stir yet.
Let warblers in the honey-locust trees
blur the obtuse tick of that clock.

Hungry Sonnet

So much hunger on the edge of bloom.
Everything yearning for its own fist of red petals.
Last year's bulb shoots out green spears
in the dark basement. My daughter retrieves her set
of water colors and the pianist in this house
can't get up from her bench, hot for the pistons
of her fingers to pump out more Bach.

Only the truly done for are spared.
A riddled walnut tree, wintry with age, never leafed out—
even this jaw-dropping May can't rouse it.
My neighbor the sculptor takes hold of a branch,
tugs and levers it, hangs her weight until it snaps.
Chisel, gouge, and mallet in her apron, she cradles
the dead thing in her arms, already peeling bark.

Kitchen Muse

Talking on his phone, a man walks by my window,
baby strapped to his chest. The baby, facing forward,

looks happy, shiny new world laid out before her,
safety at her back, but I'm thinking his call

better be important, not just to break up boredom.
Though god knows, babies

can be boring. Same game, same
need, same distraction. Same bliss too.

Wrinkled-up pleasure. Their generous eyes
and uncivilized screeches

sling arrows into our deep animal being.
I'm at the other end, old familiar world laid out

before me, less of it, memory at my back.
Some days time's door opens as I'm waking,

suspends me in the devastating gap
between a dream of what's lost and a return

to daily life. The view knocks me out.
Time, wrinkled-up pleasure.

Now I miss the baby days, squashy legs
kicking my belly, heft of a padded bottom

on my arm. I eye that man, baby bottle in hand,
while I make breakfast. What work, feeding hunger.

Soil, seeds, field hands, machinery, cows,
chickens, rain, drought, but for most of us,

just fetching and cooking. That too a day's work
if it's prolonged complexity.

Then a few minutes to devour it.
Is everything like that? A blaze of effort,

produce, people, quickly gone. I plan
to walk later in Sibley woods, let trees do

their work. Evergreens. They don't try
to tell me anything, they stand there, same place,

same rough feathers. As long as I look,
they stop time in its tracks.

Ars Poetica with Eating Utensil

Because their words had forked no lightning they
Do not go gentle into that good night.
   —Dylan Thomas

In days of innocence a fork was just a fork.
Your tiny hand lifted peas, aimed unsteadily

at an eager mouth. Later you stabbed hunks
of seared meat, consumed greedily.

On the road it became a choice. Go one way,
forget the other. Though appetizing things

lie along the other path. Then, shock, one prong
of lightning and you are so lit. You and that fork, electric.

A poem with a good aim and a mask of certainty
has a destiny like heavy pieces of silver,

scraped, bent, inscribed with initials,
handed down generation to generation.

A forked tongue sparks unpredicted fires.
You might strike, you might be struck.

Is there a choice? Shapely device of plated weight,
you only meant to ease hunger.

Starburst Sonnet

I skipped astrophysics, believing I couldn't grasp
laws of deep space, quarks and, can I say it, quirks
of early mass. Starstruck life. Just so much dark matter,
so explosive. Like tonight's wine glass when I raised
the matter of our past. It hit the floor, a hundred newborn
comets. No skipping the past. How timeless,
from the first kaboom. Who believes there's no such thing
as time? This soft body, waiting for its detonator. Stardust,
transmuted to earthly mire, stuff of cleaning day. Sweep, sweep,
wipe, wipe, as if life might sparkle like a newborn again.
As if not hearing makes it not true. Once I skipped my date
with a doctor not to hear bad news. Lived anyway,
little miracle, little starburst in my heart, little enough
to say I could have died. We'd never have known each other.

Unsilked

Cinematic and literary, I dreamed of a woman
wandering headlands in blithering fog.

She liked a bit of storm and spent her evenings
in black silk. Someone a little feral.

We'd graze each other on a crowded sidewalk,
she'd know I was the One.

In fact, we met at a late night party,
talked in the dark. She wore a t-shirt, jeans,

perched drunkenly in a tree, unsteady
as any girl on a slender pedestal.

Weeping over an ex. Next day she didn't
remember me. We both joined a women's group—

she still didn't recognize me. These women
laid out losses like exquisite rags. She left

without speaking, said later,
What kind of women do that?

Afternoon at a nude beach, the Russian River,
imagination geared up again, raced its twisted course.

I pictured heartbreak, knew I'd need something
to ease the pain. Good drugs or better lies.

In fact there was infidelity, I won't say whose,
but I wasn't ready for too much sanity.

Breakage everywhere, neither china nor glass.
We separated, linked up again, buried the past.

Unburied, buried, crime flowers planted everywhere.
What kind of women do that?

One home after another, better rugs,
a sectional sofa. A child who grew tender, feline,

winding herself between us.
We got old. Still there's a shiver, right?

The feral one molted like a winter finch.
Learned nothing except to uncover.

Feather by splendid feather,
we met at last

the intimate thing that lodges
in sleeping bodies curled around each other.

About This Pain in My Chest

Happiness, a word that begins with chance
                and ends like a kiss. Supple,
except for the *pop* at its heart. And the heart,
                frail subject, jumps off-rhythm like a jazz singer.
Prolapse, embolism, constriction. Even exertion
                is risky and anxiety drives it wild.
Yes, the heart. With a pistol or a brutal appraisal,
                it's the place to aim. It collapses and dies.
No happiness, sweet target, when I let ammunition fly
                last night. When I could sleep, I dreamed
I dumped a barrelful of fault-finding into inky water.
                Love, I slept through the cure.

Fading Sonnet

Earth sheds color as a flushed sun drops
into water. Our panorama disappears too.
We, standing apart on a bluff above the Pacific,
have nothing to look at now but silhouettes.
Staggering, swept-back cypress, just torn edges
against the sky. Offshore rocks flatten, horizontal
jags of deeper darkness. Like furious pillars,
we're implanted too, no longer speaking.
Our fights are tedious, don't you think?
The clamor of surf is even louder without light.
Why were we so intent on quarreling?
Clumsiness of words, clearer too. Twilight world,
I love you. Erasing details, making everything
uncertain, leaving us to rely on touch.

Slow Seed

Damage lies also in the pace, the cold eye,
one disaster after another. *Earthquake buries village.*
Carload of teenagers disappears on unrepaired bridge.
Wildfires in California hit eightieth day.
Monday's headlines.
Compassion peels off.

Go to the garden, plant tomato seeds, peppers.
Try to grow your latitude for grief again.

Once people endured only the nearby. A father
on the next farm lost his wife to childbirth, a small community
of mourning stepped up. One nursed the newborn,
another carried the toddler.
Casseroles, lemon cakes. They halved a smoked ham,
plowed his field. When calamity came down
there was time and help to bear its weight.

Who's built for a world's suffering?
Listen to a nurse tell how she holds a phone for hours
as dying patients FaceTime family.
Twenty in four days.
Tell me how she does this.

Practice slow. Days for a seed to unfurl a shoot,
yawn out true leaves. Stems creep upward like prayers.
Weeks to make a flower, more to shape fruit.

The organ of the heart starts
as embryonic germ. Without generosity of time,
no auricles fuse, no septa firm, no arterial stalks emerge.
No pink muscled plumpness, no steady drum.

Red Shirt

In a little mess by the front door
the silk shirt signals how kitty missed me.

Dragged from laundry basket
to where I disappeared, his token of fear,

ache of absence. His world, he tells me daily,
is me. Haunted by loss—oh, aren't we all?—

lurching toward us, glacier of devastation
poised until we stop looking.

Because I cherish you more than ever,
I have dark dreams. How did love grow like that?

Maybe time did it, the narrowed horizon.
The long alley to age relieved me

of baggage, opened my lovely armor,
nothing but cracks and crumbling left.

Cat chooses his daily totem. If it's a hard day,
a pair of pants or heavy grey hoodie gets hauled

down the stairs, through the house to that ruinous
portal. His poor teeth, his jaw pulling

such weight, dragging the thing between his legs.
See how much I missed you. See what I offer

for your return. I'd tote anything myself
if I could secure you at time's threshold.

Red scarf, heart locket, even the fleece blanket.
Snake skin, toad's foot.

Rumors of Abandonment

Each room holds a trap
where emptiness might seize. Not even the stillness

in the air seems safe: atmospheric choke before a storm.
In your study blinds are drawn,

your papers put away and I think I might go under.
Where this foolish grief comes from—

you'll be back next week—I don't know,
but the thudding in my chest is a true story.

Outside is better. I end up at a cemetery
which is sort of peopled, at least with the past.

Breeze captures confetti of blossoms and silence
delivers the missing pieces:

vacancy of long ago, not the teeming present.
Present, I can handle that.

I'm playing at a child's survival again. Thank you, I guess,
for leaving me to reunion with ghosts.

A flare-up, stunning, the way bare branches of quince
shoot out volleys of red in one day.

V

Rumors of Empty Spaces

Holes in the sky now, gaps in the ozone.
      And down the street a sinkhole caved in
as if purely exhausted. Kids ready to leap in.
          I had to use that adrenalined word: *Danger!*

When I use a spade to open
      my plot of earth, I remedy it with tea roses and maidenhair.

O holy frightening holes. Their meaning wholly
      what I was raised on. Holes in his hands and feet.
Cruelty and confusion.

      A hole here and there to be expected:
mind the gap, fill 'er up, please. But absence, piercing vacancy.
      In the kitchen I arrange plums, peaches in a bowl,
each fruit holding its own pit.

Pocket of air, cleft in the rock.
      O round sequence of mystery, circular relic, sacred cenote.
I want to fill you up, little chink in the heart.

Stormy Sonnet

Rain sheets sideways over roofs and pounds
love notes into parched dirt, sloppy kisses
to rouse its long sleep. Upstairs, I'm mesmerized
as the crown of a large oak sways. Fierce wind,
tangerine leaves sweeping dark sky,
until, across the street, an unstable Chinese elm
uproots itself, leaps onto the wet road and collapses
in a wild green shiver. Ten months, no rain.
Months, terrorized by drought, fire, heat.
We're mad for the spectacle of a storm. No power
in the neighborhood, high risk of floods
and mudslide. We're not out singing,
we're cloistered inside. But single-hearted,
devout, whispering Hallelujahs to the sky.

Incantation After a Week of Storms

Darkness lifts and I'm left in lemony light,
a body able to breathe again. Simple in and out,

no ragged throb, no churned sea.
I've lost desire, the urgent need

for the unknown thing. Yearning no longer
roils the air the way pitch of storms swept up

the yard, taking blossoms, menacing small birds
who furled their wings and bowed.

Sweet tranquility, sweet grass. Leaves shake
their soft points, slow green dancers.

Trees nod quietly, absent fragile chains
of white blossoms. Peace, leave me

a little want, pure as an adolescent buzz,
clear as tequila in a china teacup.

Stunned Sonnet

I can't resist praise again. The way its blaze
sweeps the sky. Can't stop staring, orange flame
flickering in each leaf. A tree, honestly, is a god.
All of them. They reach into the world, strip away
words. Lord over us, ignore us as gods do.
Their staggering ease of spectacle.
Even ragged and bare, forked, twisting through
grey firmament, they ravish us. Wind-blown,
lopsided as a stricken woman, burnt, scarred,
broken on barren land, they silence us.
Needled, feathered, divine green beaks pointed up.
Small lacy parasols, some, littered with blossoms.
Gods, with one commandment: whatever you do,
hold onto your ground, astound someone.

Solstice Night

Douse the lamps as snow flurries
like drowsy birds. Dream of white tulips,
white sand beaches. The world gone,
nothing mortal outside.
From night's deep bowl darkness runs over.
Mid-sleep there's a groan, lower
than human, audible through draped
windows, the dusky bellows of earth, a sound
to cover unfathomed distance: so much night,
a Neolithic cache of exposure.

Summer, when foggy bay mornings create
a grey pall, you'll cherish December.
How did desire, so mindless, get imprinted
on a chilled spread of clouds? Heat of sun
won't satisfy, not like a fire and a furnace.
Everyone goes travelling and long days
seem frivolous. Better a cold road at midnight,
the dream's cave. But that's not the reason.
You don't know the reason,
harsh and elated have become one.

Spider Season

Sticky filaments drape the path. Hairy trolls
      I try not to rile.
An orb like rings of a tree slung at my window
hangs jamb to stile. Web-light, little shimmers
in the morning.
      This afternoon, a fly and the reigning spider
scramble up the latticework to devour it.

Also the dirty season, ten months, no rain.
      Soil's grey, not a good color for dirt.
Dust films the live oaks. The weeping cherry dropped
its fruit. Lurid purple stains sidewalks
until rains come. If rains do come.
      Inside the house, everything's dulled,
strung out on solitude.

Life lost its gleam as the plague wore on.
      I'm shy of adventure, caution dug into my bones.
Shake things up, I think. Go somewhere.
Perilous, subdued self answers.
I've got a taste for comfort, the dead end
      for risk-taking. Confined animals,
we don't run when the keeper neglects to lock the cage.

Confetti Sunset

Shreds of light left.
       How do things just disappear?
A cloud loses shape. Asking is wishing
       there were answers.
What my cat thinks. Why my child's
       sometimes a stranger. How to recall
what I felt at five, shrieking and wild
       through tall grass.
Look at that sky, turning itself inside out,
       showing what lies within blue.
Everything has other sides. The way I'm relieved
       to uproot my garden in October.
I love the sprouting and fruiting. I'm done in
       by the clamoring, *pick me, cook me, eat me.*
The things that matter, all unknowable.
       How will I face dying?

VI

Incantation to Unleashing

A fevered time. Waves of heat, dread flashes—
the female body's sheet lightning.

I'm a remote star on the fade. I run the big fan
all night and God I love how its breezy fingers

ply the midnight swelter, ferry off flushed days.
Its motor, an elegant crooning thing

turning darkness around, wings that furrow air.
By morning I'm bare beneath a blanket, knees bent,

hands together, a supplicant. The rhythmic
white whirr has cut the room adrift. Airborne.

O body, and your seemingly solid hold,
just a gossamer thread tethers me.

January

Time to practice. Midwinter, your heart's clock
slows down. Your eye won't labor for small treasures,

ignoring the velvety depth of gray, fretwork
of branches against sky. It's easy to open up in April—

young sun, one blooming thing after another—
until you forget the casualties. And October's feast,

showers of red on the street, gold on the table.
Now chilled bursts of air cuff your face

and you say January's a brutalist. I say, a master class.
Out of the numbed-down life. Live at a child's pace,

dream in the languid streams of raw light.
Sprays of berries drape winter greens.

They won't last long. Neither do we for that matter.
But for a minute, be a fledgling in a breath-stopping world.

I'm not brave, just imagine wilder places, as if I might
actually go. Like the Arctic north, stripped of illusion.

It would undo the schooling to brush off extinction,
whether we survive this world. No remorse,
it kills with unbearable beauty.

Tense Sonnet

December was sultry, then came a frigid summer.
Mid-August the goldfinch started her nest. *Too late,*
I said. No use, we speak different tongues. She bent
twigs into a sturdy bowl I couldn't have made.

Smooth hands, no pincers or claws. Meant
for grabbing. Waving and pointing, helpful in foreign
places where I speak only present tense. Present,
too tense. Notions of future perfect blink in my head:

something will have saved us before our children's fate
is locked in. A fat squirrel rocks back in the tree's shade,
cleans bits of peach from hairy paws. March, it stared
at bared limbs, unable to think plenty might come.

The little finch proceeds as if she'll be fine.
I do what I can, pour seeds in a feeder I've hung.

In the Gallery of Extreme Mammals

You look endangered here, gangly upright
        species of the Anthropocene, too human next to *Thalacoleo*.
Pouch lion, half kangaroo, its bite more powerful
        than anything alive now. See how it crouches
as if to leap, seize you by the throat.

        But your kind charred its habitat millennia ago,
hunted its food out of existence. Likewise the *Uintatherium*,
        a horsey two-ton freak with drooping fangs
and bony snags on a dished-out skull.

Go ahead, gawk. *Megatherium*, giant sloth,
        tall and broad as an elephant, a gentle creature who survived
on flowers, dangles claws savage enough
        to tear you apart. Massive beasts of the Pliocene,
small of brain, lived longer than your kind.

Big red sign says No Touching. You want to touch.
        Balancing around on two limbs, you itch to graze
the domed spines, reach inside *Glyptodon*'s colossal shell,
        grasp the ghostly nothingness there.
To know what it means to vanish.
        Saber-toothed tiger, *Smilodon fatalis*—blackness
empties from its eyes.

Who'll pose you in your territory? On a couch, legs splayed,
    torso bent to the nectar of a digital screen.
Look at our squishy predecessors, androids will say.
    Kind of sweet, weren't they?

Destroyed Sonnets

1

Indiscreet creatures rustle in damp grass
and a screech owl, rapturous, readies her throat.
Half moon, half-lit sky, half-lost, already old
when poppies open, spiky cordgrass shakes off dew.
Human voices return, nine big cars for fourteen people.
Unnoticed by the crew: a bobcat skittering off.
Tourists we are, crossing salt marshes to get to the beach,
giants treading delicate flora, whooping laughter
like children on holiday. What's a jeweled snake,
a bush rabbit breakfasting on pink stalks of verbena,
the rare red fox to partygoers? A man cracks open
the cooler for his first beer, another drops a cellophane
wrapper behind a dune, then tosses a stick at gulls
grabbing his potato chips. Gulled ourselves.

2

Gulls grab potato chips. Gulled ourselves,
believing we snatch what we want with impunity.
Molten air, early days of the coming heat.
Where to go but beaches? Everything glitters—
sand, ground quartz, and glass—the fine crush burns.
Six foot waves, salty jeweled sovereigns,
collapse into foam. Sun torches overhead. We won't
survive this, will we? Slow disappearance,
voices fading, eons of trash giving itself back.
We'll take much of the wild with us, flora and fauna.
Hush will reign. Imagine the far future,
fresh gust of air, brown death slowly greening.
Small things winging dense fog at dawn.
Indiscreet creatures rustling in damp grass.

Ars Poetica as Conundrum

How to love a blooming orchard
if you won't eat its sour apples.

To ask for scented roses if you hate
the shit it feeds on. You know a pond streaked

with moonlight hides a skirt of peagreen scum.
October sun warms your hands

while it curls and yellows these pages.
Like poems that go wrong before

you finish them. Where were you headed
the lines tried to follow. You came

to a dead end. Or some indifferent door
to revelation. What does perfection feel like

and how many are its flaws. How do you love
a God if you can't stand His disciples.

Rumors of the Great Change

Some applauded it, convinced it
would do the trick, take us back to what once
      kept us alive, nursed the heart and bone of us.
Revelation without words, since we roll over
      each others' words.
In disaster is the only hope, they said,
      ignoring how fear makes devils of us.
Shuts our eyes to what binds us together.
      It prefers armies. Look how far fear's disciples
have gone, more lost than the rest of us.
      It's a blaze in the spine, an all night vigil
on catastrophe. We're frail after all.
      Fear of this world grips us—the icy burial
of winter, the blister of sun. Acres of forest
      buckle under fire and storms blow
great houses apart. What are we doing
      on this wild planet? Our only home,
with the sweetness of common sparrows. I wonder,
      does the earth still want us?
Now we ask: will calamity sing down the angels?
      Only if the holy quota of fear holds tight.

Green Sonnet

Days spill off the loom: wouldn't have guessed
life could be this smooth in a calamitous time.
Days so sweet they beg for gratitude.
I've stopped hounding the scent of suffering,
I know I'm blessed, know trauma's at the gate,
but I have a good woman with me
and moments to take pleasure
where we can, even in sorrow's dark thimble:
what other antidote to anguish?
I won't wear my mourning cloak, I've slung it
over the lawn chair. Heavy old worsted thing
I don't need in this weather. In the garden
a wall of *podocarpus* screens the yard.
Sweep of green, breeze slinking like a cat.

Messenger

She stands at my door without knocking.
No one knocks any more. Friends gone
to remote screens, neighbor fixed to her stoop
as the dog pees, cloaked faces passing by.
Even packages, just a thud.

Days melt into night. Moths flutter at windows,
my cat paws glass. There's a horror out there,
but I only know the shaky mysteries of silence.

Slowly earth greens. Deer and quail come down
from the hills. Look, three goldfinch in the lavender,
female and two males, a clean triangle of bird.
One flies to the lemon tree, blends into fruit.
The female flits to the naked gingko, bold little diva.
Quick swoops and they're off. February, so early
for the mating game. Have all the rules changed?

When I sleep, the girl's there again and her cryptic smile.
My red door glows, a bauble under porch light.
Her dress the cobalted sky of the Sierra, how city sky
looks now, lacking its smudge. What does she want?
Message unspoken. Does she stand at the door
of every dream, wait for us to wake up?

Acknowledgments

Grateful thanks to the editors of the following journals for publishing these poems.

Ascent: "Incantation Against Blazing"

Bateau: "Rumors of the Old Somewhere"

Barrow Street: "Kitchen Muse," "Rumors of the Solitary Pulse," "Unsilked"

Bracken: "Hollow Bones," "Stormy Sonnet"

California Quarterly: "Mortal Absence"

Catamaran: "Elegy with Bereft Cat"

Chicago Quarterly Review: "Rumors of Empty Spaces"

The Cortland Review: "Incantation After a Week of Storms"

Cumberland River Review: "January"

Denver Quarterly: "Incantation for a Hard Rain"

Grist: "Sonnet on the Edge"

Guesthouse: "Destroyed Sonnet"

Gulf Coast: "Busted Sonnet"

The Hunger: "Messenger"

The Los Angeles Review: "Ars Poetica as Conundrum"

Mudlark: "Rumors of the Great Change," "Solstice Night," "Tense Sonnet"

North Dakota Quarterly: "Red Shirt," "Rumors of Abandonment"

On the Seawall: "Autobio in Scent Memory," "Post Haste," "Slow Seed"

Rhino: "Restless Sonnet"

Smartish Pace: "Born-Again Sonnet"

Southern Poetry Review: "Seven A.M."

The Southern Review: "Ars Poetica with Eating Utensil"

Swwim: "Incantation to Unleashing"

32 Poems: "Riddle"

West Trestle Review: "Uncertain Sonnet"

So much gratitude! Putting this work together leaves me very appreciative of the community of friends and writers who support me, read poems, help me know when they are ready to be a book. Special thanks goes to my writing group: Idris Anderson, George Higgins, Julia Levine, Robert Thomas, Jeanne Wagner, and Steven Winn. These amazing poets are extraordinary readers, giving exquisite attention to the line without losing sight of the whole. Traci Brimhall's reading of an early version offered a mirror necessary to understand where the poems were going. I have had many teachers of poetry in my life, including my beloved first, the late Elizabeth Phillips, who taught me how to get inside a piece of writing. As someone who went the MA route, rather than the MFA route, I was a reader before I was a writer, a practice that has enriched my life for decades.

Special thanks to Ellie Waxman whose photographic composition created a gorgeous cover and to Jeanine Chappell who made it work. I am grateful to Diane Lockward for selecting this book and guiding it to publication. Dearest thanks to Linda O'Brien and Ana O'Brien Burch, always.

About the Author

Beverly Burch is the author of four poetry collections, including *Latter Days of Eve*, which won the John Ciardi Poetry Prize from BkMk Press, and *Sweet to Burn*, which won the the Gival Poetry Prize and the Lambda Literary Award. She has also written two books on psychoanalytic theory and women's sexual/gender identifications: *On Intimate Terms* (University of Illinois Press) and *Other Women* (Columbia University Press). She lives in Oakland, California.

www.beverlyburch.com